TH   Y
Englsnd's Prayer

First published in association with the Isle of Wight Catholic History Society iow-chs.org.

© 2018 ST PAULS PUBLISHING

ST PAULS by Westminster Cathedral
Morpeth Terrace, Victoria, London SW1P 1EP
Ph: +44 (0) 207 828 5582, www.stpauls.org.uk

St Pauls Publishing
Moyglare Road, Maynooth, Co. Kildare, Ireland
Ph: +353 (1) 628 5933, www.stpauls.ie

Extracts from the Letters of TS Eliot & the Letters of Ted Hughes used with kind permission of their publishers Faber & Faber Ltd.

ISBN: 978-1-910365-41-0

Designed by MIDDLEDOT
Printed by Melita Press, Malta

ST PAULS is an activity of the priests and brothers of the Society of St Paul who proclaim the Gospel through the media of social communication.

CONTENTS

Foreword	5
Introduction	7
Joyful Mysteries	9
Luminous Mysteries	21
Sorrowful Mysteries	33
Glorious Mysteries	45
England: the Dowry of Mary	56

Foreword

Jesus Christ is the centre of our Christian Faith.

He is God the Son made man. He was born in time to reveal to us the truth about God and about how to live a happy human life. He invites us one day to live with Him forever in heaven. The Rosary is a wonderful meditation on all these basic truths of faith: the birth of Jesus, the death of Jesus for us and for our salvation, and his glorious resurrection. We pray these prayers with Mary, His Mother. I commend this booklet to you with its beautiful illustrations and inspiring thoughts. May it help you to love Jesus more and to spread that love to others, especially the poorest.

His Lordship, Monsignor Philip Egan,
Bishop of Portsmouth

In Corde Jesu + Philip

Introduction

The Rosary is an ancient Christian prayer, traditionally given to St Dominic in the 13th century by the Virgin Mary.

It is embedded in English Life as the Statutes of Eton College 1440 show: scholars were required to recite every day (using beads): 'the complete psalter of the Blessed Virgin, consisting of a Credo, fifteen Paters (Our Father) and one hundred and fifty Ave Marias (Hail Mary)'

England from ancient times was devoted to the Virgin Mary. It was known as "The Dowry of Mary" that is the place set apart for her use alone. It was formally dedicated to her in Richard II's reign, a royal dedication never since revoked. Mary's consent at the Annunciation, to be the mother of God's son, was her exercise of free will, that liberty to choose, that England has upheld down the ages against all attempts at tyranny.

This long established devotion of the Rosary was targeted in the XVIth century in the injunctions of Queen Elizabeth I in 1559:

> III… and that works devised by man's fantasies, besides scripture (as wandering of pilgrimages, setting up of candles, praying upon beads or such like superstition)

have not only no record in Scripture for doing them, but contrariwise great threatenings and maledictions of God . XXIII… that they shall take away … utterly extinct and destroy so that there remain no memory of the same.

This collection of modern poems, pictures old and new, and quotations from history show that the Rosary, despite all attempts to suppress it, remained and remains "England's Prayer".

THE JOYFUL MYSTERIES

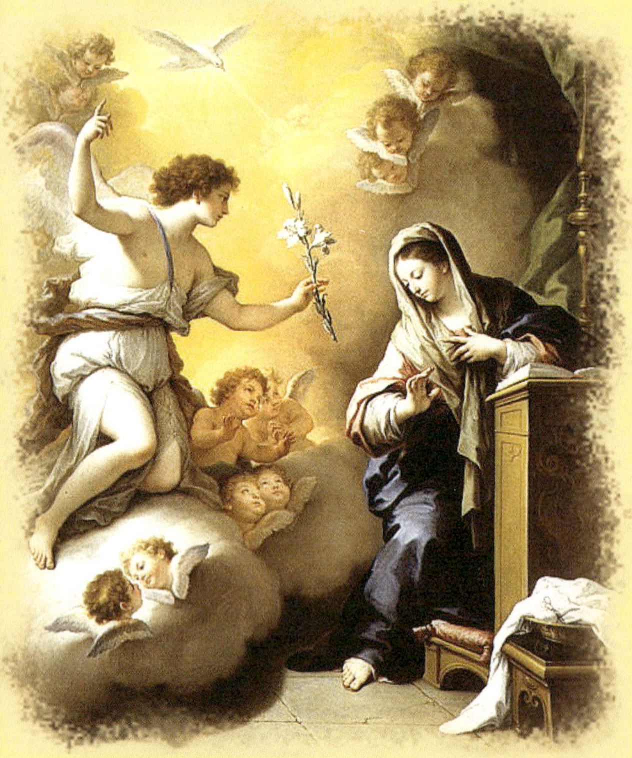

1. The Annunciation

Silent whispers in an uncurled ear
A shaft of light
Announces
Strikes without sound to the core's consent
A lift of sight
Awe stirs in an amazed womb

Of small coral about her arm she bare
A pair of beads gauded all with green

Canterbury Tales
Geoffrey Chaucer 1343-1400

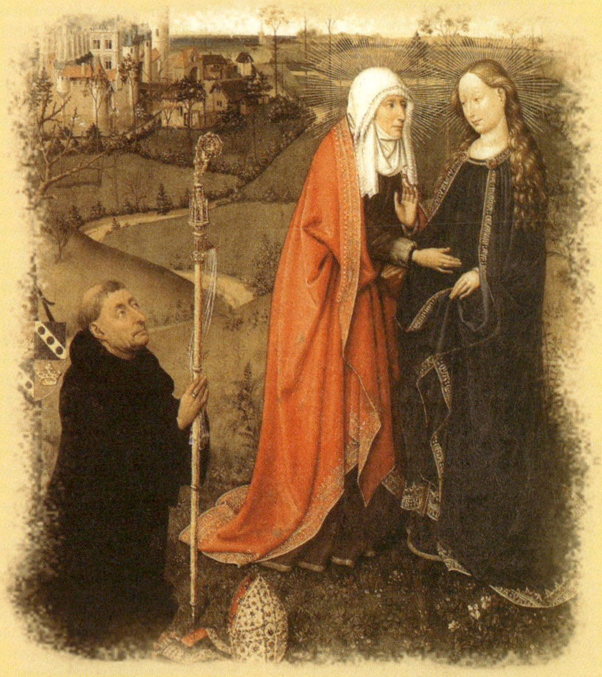

2. The Visitation

The hill country of Judaea is dry
And at this season drier
Than sand with no sea.
Parched,
The desert possesses
The arid soil as wind
Whips up grains that sting the eye and score
The cheek with lacerations.
Skin shrinks from its contact like a child from
harsh words.

Hurrying, she comes heavily along the goat path
To greet her cousin. Suddenly,
A kick of life; the baptist struggles
To erupt on Jordan's banks as Elizabeth
Staggers into words and hails with praise.

Commend thy grievance to my holy prayers
For I will be thy beadsman, Valentine.

Two Gentlemen of Verona – Act 1 Sc 1
William Shakespeare 1564-1616

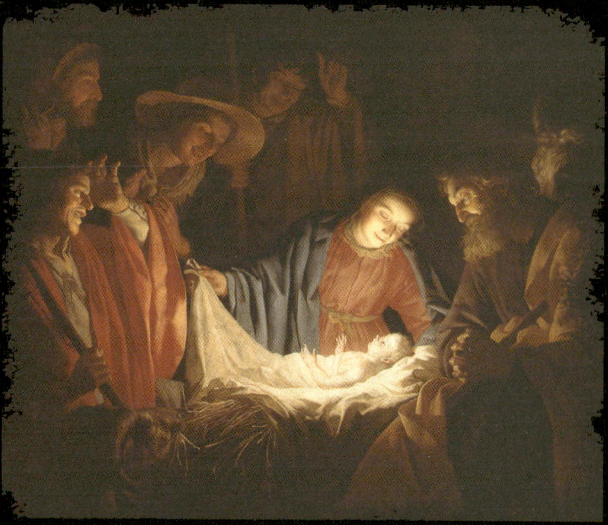

3. The Nativity

Cradling and enclosing arms
Rock the child. Voices
Pass by outside. It's quiet,
The sounds of day dying in the night.
Inside, nothing but simplicity
A mother, child.
No wild prophesyings,
No outflung arm declares
Here! The Messiah!

Hush; it's only a world that has not woken;
Stars at their stations, shepherds yet to come.

All night she spent in bidding of her bedes,
And all the day in doing good and godly deedes.

Faerie Queen
Edmund Spenser 1552-1599

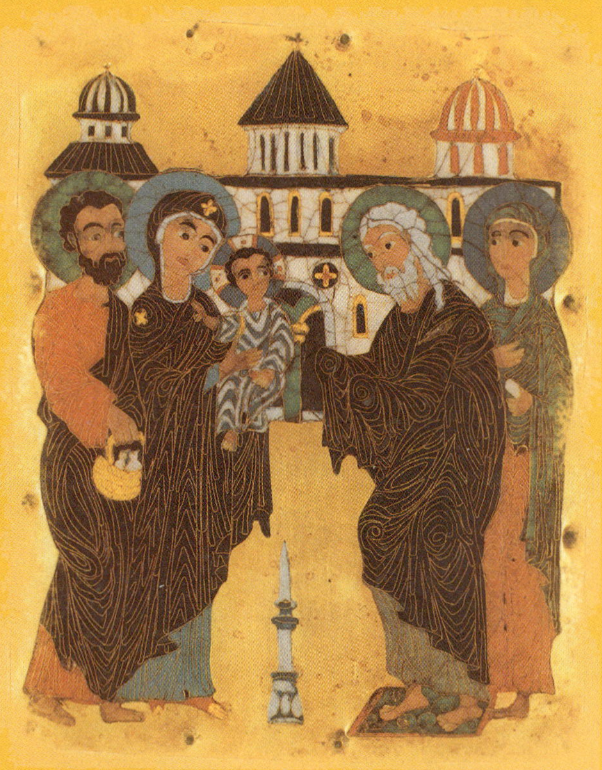

4. The Presentation in the Temple

The temple, bright with stone,
Reflects the morning sun.

Simeon wakes to another day of prayer.
He senses he must go.
So many times this slight
Inclination, this soft
Pressing on the will.
He can refuse, he can abjure....

He hurries through the streets
To greet priests and people, then stops.
"Who is that woman?" wanting no grace
To set off form and face…

Light breaks through his patient heart. At last.

In simple kindness he lifts her child to bless.
The priest quiets her unrest
Prompted by a prophecy that speaks of spears.

When holy and devout religious men
Are at their beads, 'tis hard to draw them thence,
So sweet is zealous contemplation.

King Richard III Act1 Sc7
William Shakespeare 1564-1616

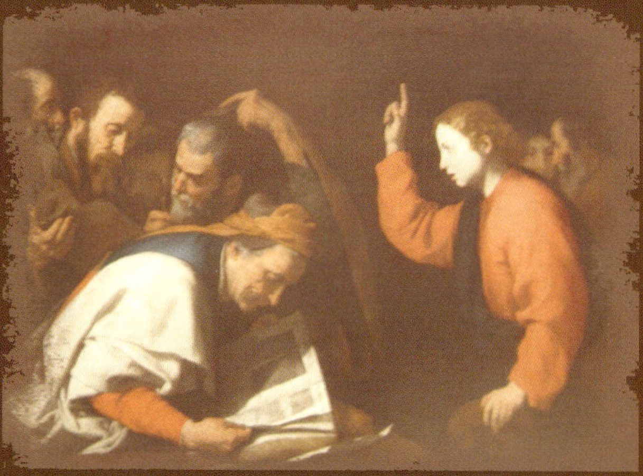

5. The Finding of Jesus in the Temple

"Where were you?
Your father, I, spent three days.
How could you neglect
Your first concern? What could they learn
From a child of twelve?"

Then she remembered
The amazed expression on the men's faces.
She held him close, but could not stop
Her arms trembling.

Now the great power of the Rosary lies in this, that it makes the Creed into a prayer; of course the Creed is in some sense a prayer and a great act of homage to God; but the Rosary gives us the great truths of his life and death to meditate upon, and brings them nearer to our hearts.

John Henry Newman 1801-1890

THE LUMINOUS MYSTERIES

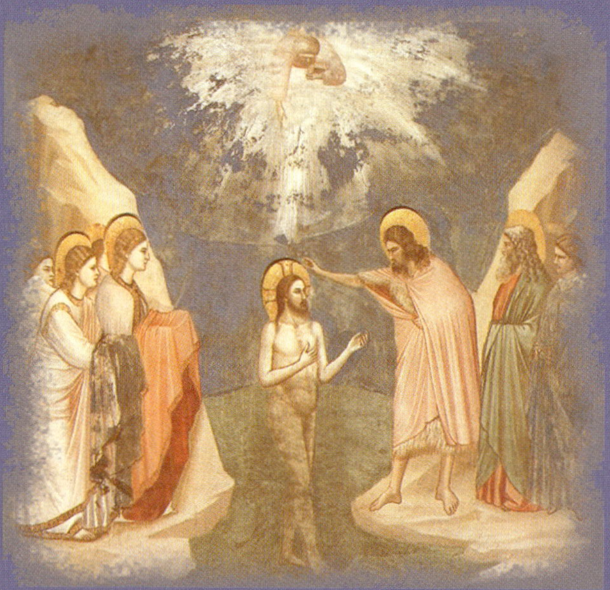

1. The Baptism of the Lord

The angled light
Endlessly reflecting
Made the uncertain movement of the waters
A dance of joy.

His shadow fell from the morning sun.

The busy man, intoning, crying, praising –

"John!" He shadowed his eyes to cry: "I am not fit".

But his cousin's command let him part the waters.
The river flowed to heaven. Heaven replied.

O, for my beads! I cross me for a sinner.

Comedy Of Errors Act 2 Sc 2
William Shakespeare 1564-1616

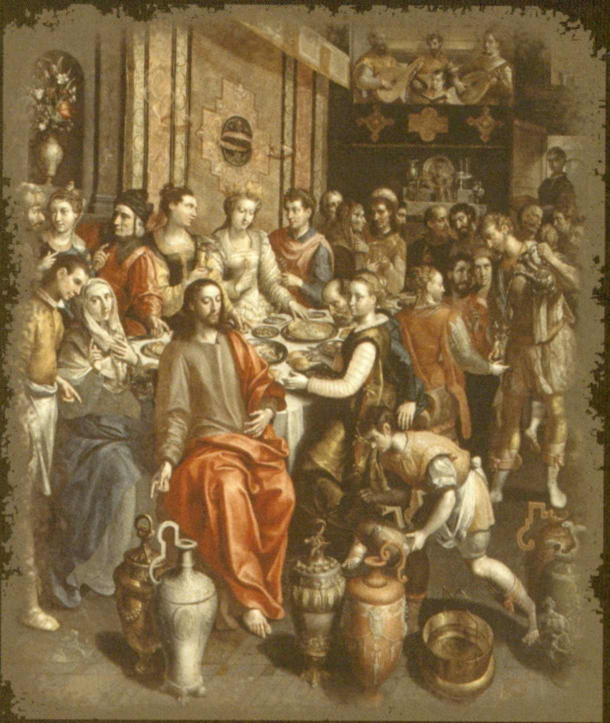

2. The Wedding Feast at Cana

Bustling servants annoyed the bridal host.
He wished the best and this sudden scurrying,
The turned eyes, unsettled him.

His daughter, his beloved daughter,
Must not have a moment mar her day.
What are these servants so anxious for?
He saw their eyes and followed them
Past the table lovingly prepared
Past his proud family
Past the bowls of fruit, of meat, of cheese
Past the cups
To the quiet group and the quiet admonishment
He missed, but saw its astounding outcome.

And the vessels of his daughter's wedding overflowed
With a wine whose majesty taste alone could not convey.

When the Museum of London carried out the excavation work, the staff found many objects which are now stored in the museum itself. One of the most suggestive artefacts was the fragment of a rosary made of bone with copper alloy links… dated 1550-1600.

Rose Theatre, Bankside 1587-1606
Excavated 1989

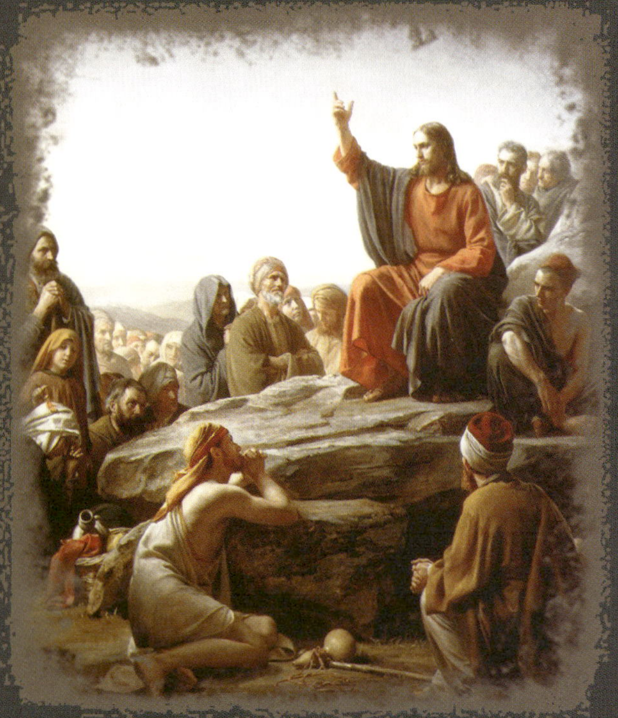

3. The Proclamation of the Kingdom

The carpenter's tools were ready
When the news of his cousin came
She saw him listen intently
But his look was not the same
As the beloved son at supper
The touch on his father's plane

He took off the carpenter's apron
He asked for water and bowl
He washed his arms to the elbow
He dried with the usual towel
But his look was not the same
As he passed down the hall

She saw him by the seashore
She heard him on the hill
The look on his listeners' faces
Told her he was still
Her beloved son, now doing
With words his father's will.

And so the babe grew up a pretty boy,
A pretty boy, but most unteachable –
And never learnt a prayer, nor told a bead

The Foster-Mother's Tale
Samuel Taylor Coleridge 1772-1834

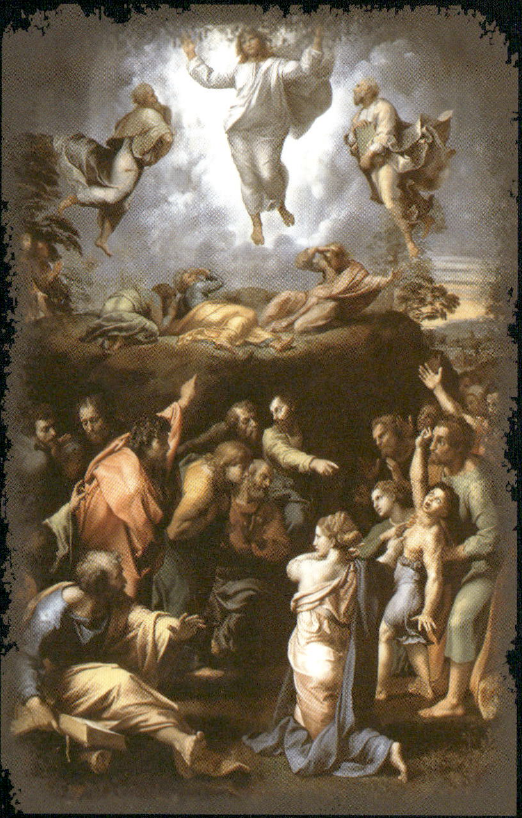

4. The Transfiguration

They could not see
In the pure light where there was only light
Dazzling, beyond vision

Amazement alone let them see

....

Where were they?

Suddenly he was there again
Familiar, unsettling, beloved.

Where were the men? The voice?
What had happened?
The light, the light was all they could remember.

He told them not to be afraid.

*...wende to holi chirche,
And there bidde my bedes,*

Piers Plowman
William Langland. c 1332-1386

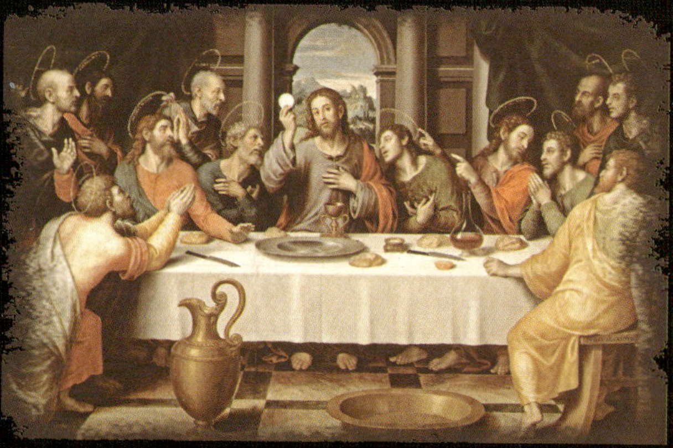

5. The Eucharist

If I could catch the morning,
Cup it in my hands and spin it
Like a globe of sparkling glass,
I could not image grace –
Clear as a silver line
Or bright like the sun
Yet here to eat – a white wafer of light
Dissolving
On the tongue like dew.

To love and to be grieved befits a dove
Silently telling her bead-history:
Trust all to Love, be patient and approve:
Love understands the mystery.

Judge Nothing before the Time
Christina Rossetti 1830-1894

THE SORROWFUL MYSTERIES

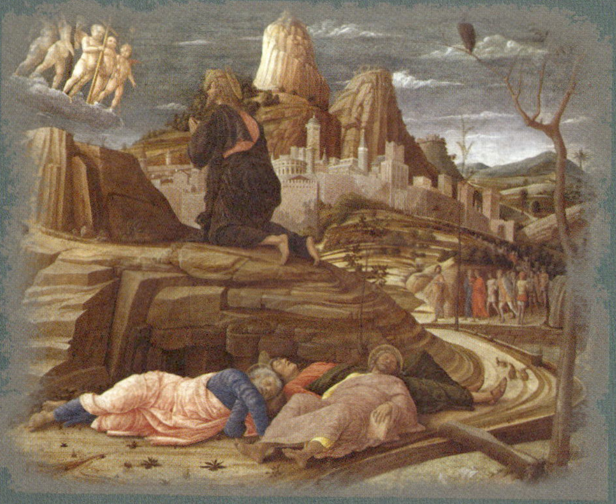

1. The Agony in the Garden

He does not notice
Peter fall asleep
Andrew
John

The clicking cicada chorus in shrill chant.
It's warm.
Passover wine fumes their senses like a drug.

"I ask only that it be
According to your ...
I do not understand.
I do not."

Centuries of sin appear.
He breathes, hearing himself breathe,
Hearing his heart beat.
"I must bear"

Sweat breaks out in drops
That stain the thirsty ground
"If it must be done.
If this cup -
Father.." And Son.

Shall we go throw away our coats of steel,
And wrap our bodies in black mourning gowns,
Numbering our Ave-Maries with our beads?

King Henry 6th Act2 Sc1
William Shakespeare 1564-1616

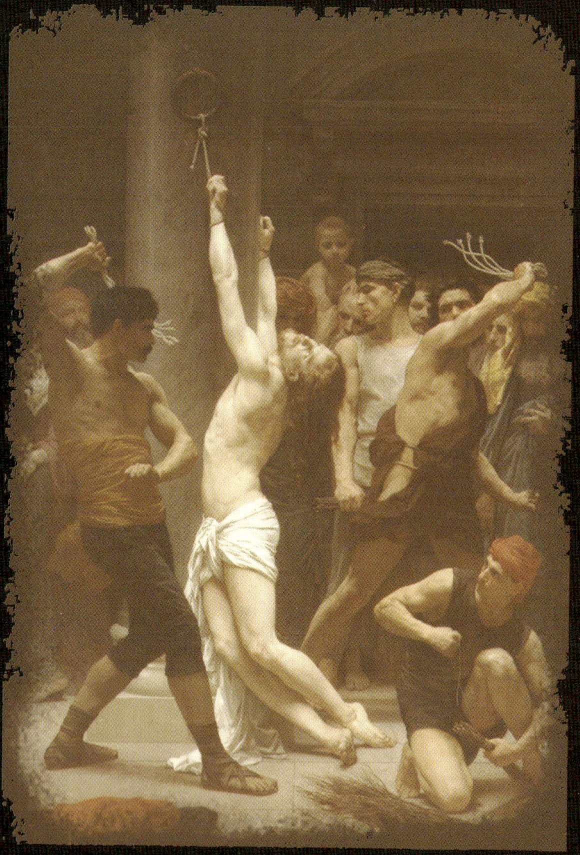

2. The Scourging at the Pillar

He is tied to the pillar in full view.
Citizens shy away.
Soldiers
Crack almonds and cry out in scorn.

It's not the first lash.
It's when, lash on lash,
There's no skin left to break;
When the back
Is one raw mass of flesh.

He stands shaking.
He tries with psalms to hold back the pain.

Behold the child, by Nature's kindly law,
Pleased with a rattle, tickled with a straw:
Scarves, garters, gold, amuse his riper stage,
And beads and prayer-books are the toys of age:

An Essay on Man: Epistle II
Alexander Pope 1688-1744

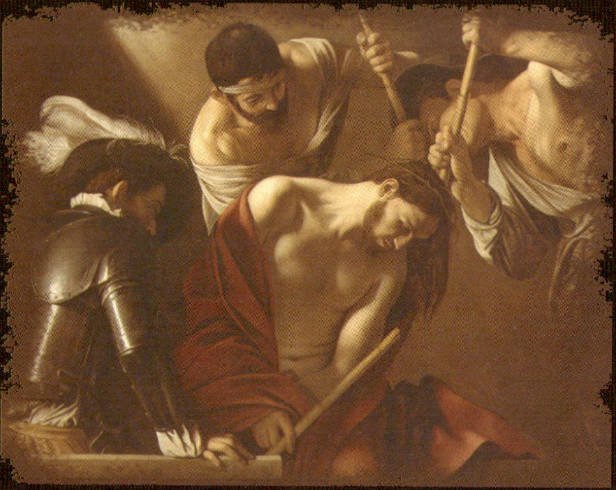

3. The Crowning with Thorns

The soldier pricked thumb and forefinger
Trying to mould
Intransigent stems
Into a wound circlet.
The purple cloth his robe.
The reed his sceptre.

"Hail, King of the Jews"

Crowned
With a thrust of thorns.
Blood trickles down his face.
They clown, mocking, mocking,
While his head holds
Its sign of kingship......the kingdom yet to come.

...it probably requires a note to say that the decades of the rosary are 15, 5 Joyful, 5 Sorrowful, 5 Glorious...I know all about the decades of the rosary

Letter to Thomas McGreevy 1928
TS Eliot 1888-1965

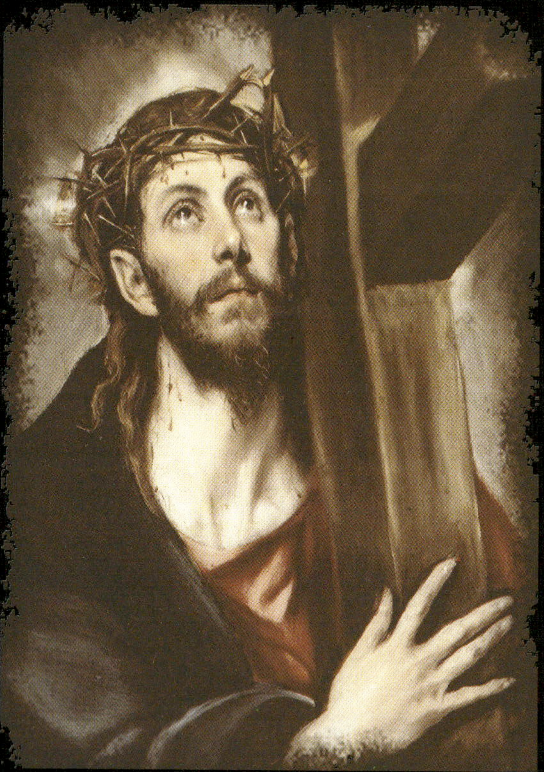

4. The Carrying of the Cross

He staggers, falls, is summoned
By rough hands to stand.
"Simon from Cyrene"
Blood films his eyes.
"Veronica"
He falls again.
The crowd jostles close
Some silent, others shouting.
"O Daughters of Jerusalem.."
"Mind"
It is weighted.
The coarse cross-piece
Lodges splinters in his back.

His mother stands,
Seeing his lifted eyes,
Unable to look away.
He mounts the path up the darkening hill.

She then rose and dried her eyes, and taking a crucifix from her neck offered it to me.
She saw, I suppose, the doubt in my face, for she put the rosary round my neck and said, "For your mother's sake," and went out of the room.
I am writing up this part of the diary whilst I am waiting for the coach, which is, of course, late; and the crucifix is still round my neck.

Dracula Chapter 1
Bram Stoker 1847-1912

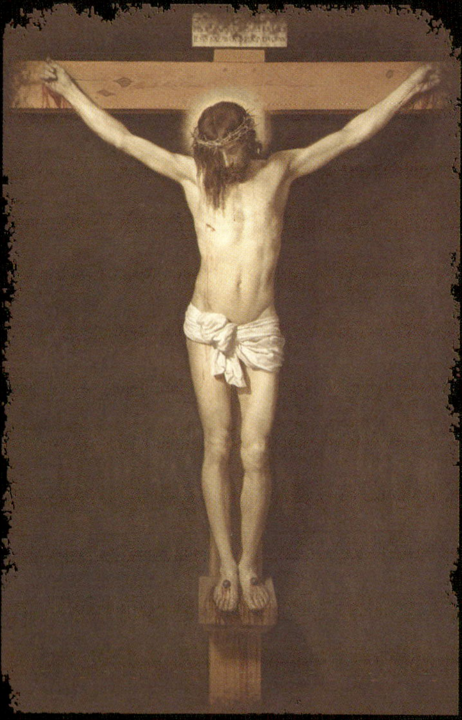

5. The Crucifixion

The nails are driven deep.
Hammering breaks the flesh.
He flinches.
The executioner goes about his work.
The wood is hauled upright,
Dropped into place. He screams.

He hangs, trying to breathe,
Unable to breathe,
Having to lunge for air, to heave up and down.

He hears the thieves.
"Water, water"
They bring vinegar.

Three hours.
A spear opens up the end. The wound gapes.
The temple splits in two.

A body hangs there, still.

"My sensibility was formed by the dolorous murmurings of the rosary"

Interview 1979
Seamus Heaney 1939-2013

THE GLORIOUS MYSTERIES

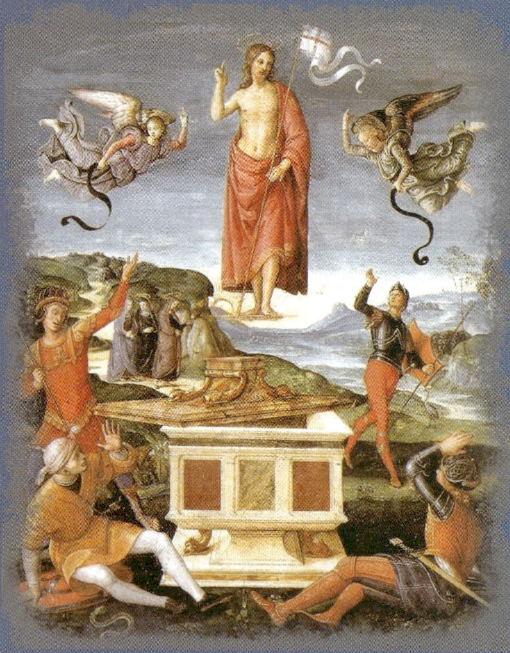

1. The Resurrection

The stone moved,
The tomb empty,
The cloths unwound, being stared at by six eyes.

Two run
And stumble down rocks.
One stays to learn
Whose heart cannot contain
Its shock of joy.

She scrambles down the path to tell the waking world.

… in the drawer of the headmaster's desk at the Leys School, Cambridge (A Methodist Foundation) there is a treasured relic which bears the tag 'John Wesley's Rosary'.

John Wesley 1703-1791

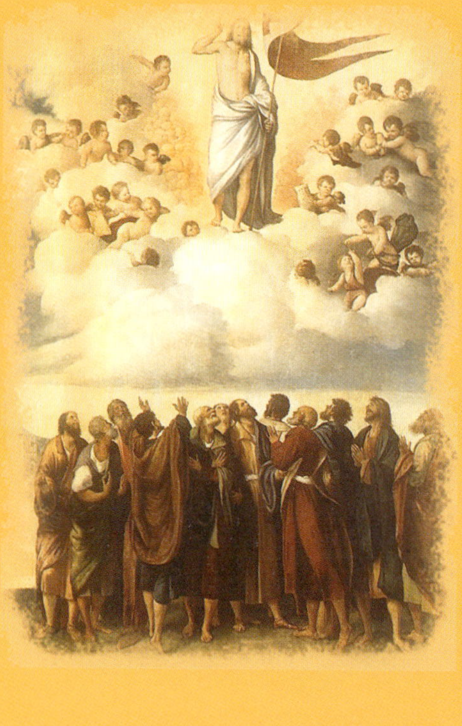

2. The Ascension

Gathered on the hill –
"Is it time?
The kingdom? The Romans?
Will Israel arise?"

"Jerusalem, Judaea, Samaria
To the utmost ends of the earth"

"And will Israel….?"

"Hush. Sheathe your swords,
Unbuckle
Belt and leather scabbard,
Learn new life"

Ascending
To draw all men up with him in love

"I found another dead badger the other day – skin no good but I am getting its teeth for my rosary"

Letter to Gerald Hughes 1969
Ted Hughes 1930-1998

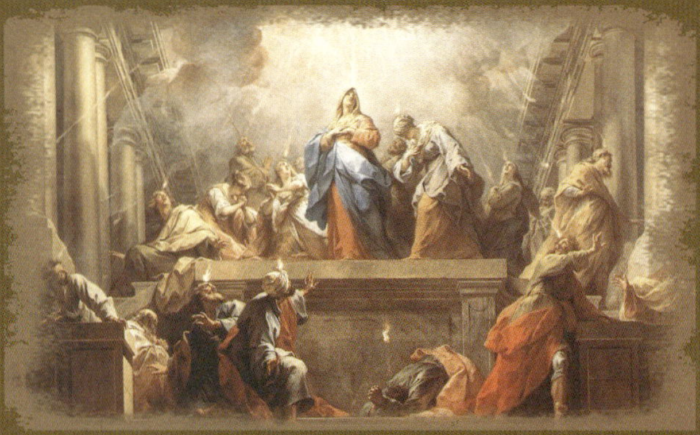

3. The Descent of the Holy Spirit

Uncertain in thought,
In hope unclear,
Frightened,
Hearing the menace of the crowd outside

"Was that the door?"
"I thought you bolted it."
"The stairs?"
"What is that sound?"

Like water, like waves

"Is he coming?"

But the mighty wind swept down the doors
Shattered doubt to break creation free
From its confinement, sending them to surge
Out into history baptised with fire.

And on the tables every clime and age
Jumbled together; celts and calumets,
Claymore and snowshoe, toys in lava, fans
Of sandal, amber, ancient rosaries,

> The Princess Prologue
> *Alfred, Lord Tennyson 1809-1892*

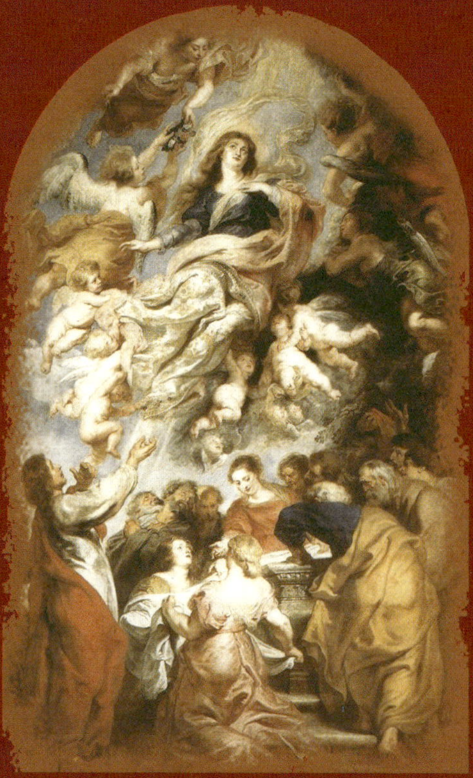

4. The Assumption

Aromatic, fragrant spices,
An anointing,
A white winding sheet,
Women weeping.

Ephesus is a warm town in summer,
Bright with washing while its children
Kick dry wine-skins down its dusty streets.

They wait, taking turns
To carry messages to John.

"Not long now. Please,
Leave me to sleep.
I can sleep now.
All I see
The sunlit yard,

The rooftops,
The sky, the blue sky"

Numb were the Beadsman's fingers, while he told
His rosary, and while his frosted breath,
Like pious incense from a censer old,
Seem'd taking flight for heaven, without a death,
Past the sweet Virgin's picture…..

St Agnes' Eve
John Keats 1795-1821

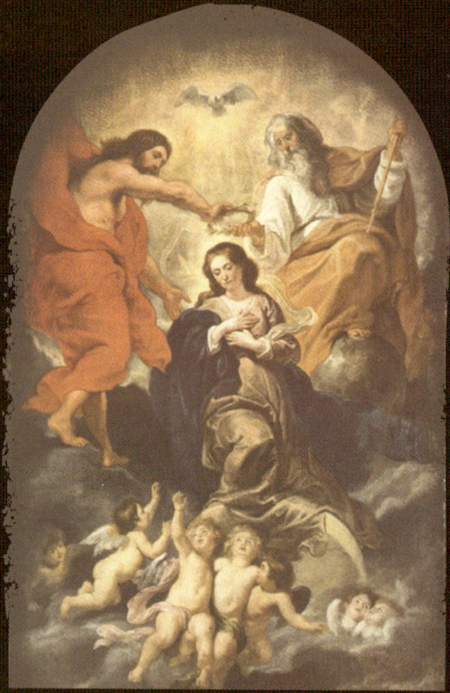

5. The Coronation of Our Lady in Heaven and the Glory of God in all His Saints

They see a city that is their own.
Light streams down the streets.
A sweet air
Sifts out the scent of spring.

What is this procession?
Yes, it's May. The crocus has flowered;
Now almond buds
Burst into blossom.

See, they return,
The lost tribes, the crew that spent its strength,
This winding chorus of praise that sings
Hallelujah! The queen is crowned
To walk abroad in the glory of God's saints.

I'll give my jewels for a set of beads,
My gorgeous palace for a hermitage,
My gay apparel for an almsman's gown,
My figured goblets for a dish of wood,
My sceptre for a palmer's walking staff,
My subjects for a pair of carved saints,
And my large kingdom for a little grave…

King Richard II Act3 Sc3
William Shakespeare 1564-1616

England as the Dowry of Mary

The dedication of England as "Mary's Dowry" – dowry here having its ancient legal sense, linked to "dower house", as the "dos" (Latin) or gift, that part of a man's estate set apart for his widow's use alone – emerges in documentary form in the 14th century. It was even then considered of "common parlance" (Archbishop Arundel 1399).

It is referred to explicitly in the Pynson Ballad of the 15th century, published by Henry VII's printer, Richard Pynson:

> *O Englonde, great cause thou haste glad for to be,*
> *To be called in every realme and regyon*
> *The holy lande, Oure Ladyes dowre;*
> *Thus arte thou named of olde antyquyte.*

The Pynson Ballad recounts the founding in 1061 of what is now the National Shrine of Our Lady in England at Walsingham, Norfolk. Walsingham before its suppression in 1538 was one of the four major pilgrimage shrines in Christendom, with Rome, Jerusalem, Santiago de Compostela. It was the only one dedicated to the Virgin Mary. The shrine was restored in 1897.

Walsingham commemorates the Annunciation, that supreme act of consent whereby Mary became the mother of God's incarnate Son. It is known as "England's Nazareth".

England as Mary's Dowry is here to incarnate the values of her Son's kingdom, a kingdom of truth and justice, of liberty and law, where peace may prevail, and freedom of choice, as Mary exercised at the Annunciation, is forever upheld.

This blessed plot, this earth, this realm, this England.

Richard II Act 2 Sc 1
William Shakespeare 1564–1616